Mindful Coloring

Mindful Coloring

CALMING THE MIND THROUGH ART

DIANA ELISABETH DUBE

INTRODUCTION BY DANIEL J. SIEGEL, MD

W. W. Norton & Company

Independent Publishers Since 1923

New York · London

For information about permission to reproduce selections from this book, write to
Permissions, W. W. Norton & Company, Inc., 500 Fifth Avenue, New York, NY 10110

For information about special discounts for bulk purchases, please contact
W. W. Norton Special Sales at specialsales@wwnorton.com or 800-233-4830

Manufacturing by R R Donnelley Harrisonburg
Book design by Molly Heron
Production manager: Christine Critelli

ISBN: 978-0-393-71178-3 (pbk.)

W. W. Norton & Company, Inc., 500 Fifth Avenue, New York, N.Y. 10110
www.wwnorton.com

W. W. Norton & Company Ltd., Castle House, 75/76 Wells Street, London W1T 3QT

1 2 3 4 5 6 7 8 9 0

For Deborah, my knight in dented armor.

Introduction

Daniel J. Siegel, MD

Founding Editor, Norton Series on Interpersonal Neurobiology
Founding Co-Director, UCLA Mindful Awareness Research Center
Executive Director, Mindsight Institute
Author, *The Mindful Brain*; *The Mindful Therapist*; and *Mind*

WHEN WE FOCUS our attention on our inner sensations, we open an important window into the world of bodily wisdom with its gut feelings and heartfelt sensibilities. As we focus attention on the nonverbal world of color and form, we also access aspects of our mental life often hidden beneath the barrage of logic and language that, for many of us, have dominated our days of schooling and beyond, shaping how we perceive the world, and even experience our sense of self.

With Diana Dube's marvelous collection of line drawings here in *Mindful Coloring*, you are invited to develop aspects of your own neural circuitry that may have been lying dormant, or at least underutilized, up until now.

In my own life's journey, finding time to get in touch with an inner compass that can guide how I draw and color helped me learn how to feel an impulse that, without logic or reason, would direct how I would reach for certain hues or was attracted to certain lines and shadings, helping access a part of my own mind that school never seemed to cultivate.

In modern neuroscience, we now know that

where attention goes, neural firing flows. And with recent discoveries in the field neuroplasticity, we also can see that how you use your mind's attention stimulates neuronal activation and growth, "SNAGging" the brain in ways that can be helpful in our well-being.

When we learn how to develop mindful awareness, studies reveal we are harnessing important connections in the brain that support neural integration—how we link differentiated regions and their functions to each other. Our "connectome" is more interconnected, and our integrative corpus callosum, hippocampus and prefrontal regions are each shown to grow with mindfulness practice. With this research we can now simply say that mindfulness integrates the brain. Getting beneath words and accessing our inner sensations while staying aware of what is happening—without judgment and expectation—is at the heart of what being mindful is all about.

This book can help you have fun while strengthening your capacity to be mindful. How? As you feel yourself drawn to a certain figure in this book, as you reach for a particular set of colors, as you carefully attend to filling in the intricate spaces between the lines, and as you

experience simply being aware without judgment, you will be immersed in the fundamental aspects of being mindful. Practicing a mindfulness exercise creates a state of mindful awareness that with time can become a trait in your life.

Well, you might be asking, why shouldn't I simply meditate? And if drawing is so helpful, why not simply doodle my way along a blank page? These are great ideas, too!

What Diana's wonderful drawings offer you is a simple invitation to be mindful in drawing. Just as in other mindfulness practices such as yoga, if you lose attention, you lose your balance. Here too, if you lose your focus of attention, you'll color over the intricate lines that make up each drawing. Staying balanced will encourage you to stay focused as well as open, the basics of mindfulness practice and mindful living.

This coloring book does not replace something else you might choose to do, it simply is a useful practice in and of itself—useful, and enjoyable. Sometimes it is helpful to keep in mind that when we live mindfully, when we immerse ourselves in a wide range of experiences filled with open awareness and close attention to what is happening as it arises, we continue to strengthen our capacity to be more fully aware, more fully present in life.

This book's drawings are a great place to begin.

In our busy modern lives, often so much of what we focus on doing is part of a "to-do" list that seems endless, with emails evoking a sense of insufficient time, always being "behind," and the Internet being really an "InfiNet" that goes on forever, rarely offering a sense of completion. *Mindful Coloring* is one antidote to this common stress and modern madness.

There is nothing to "accomplish" in these pages but to be with your inner experience and the emerging colors that come from you as you open your awareness and focus your attention on bringing them to life. Being aware within the act of coloring, a way of being which has no aim but to be with the images, focusing on the lines, enjoying the process and the emerging contours of color, is a gift of mindful awareness you can give yourself.

If you reflect on all the ways that studies now reveal mindfulness practice improves our physical and mental well-being, then you'll perhaps sense the power of such a choice to simply mindfully be in our busy lives. This is an empowering gift that keeps on giving. Enjoy!

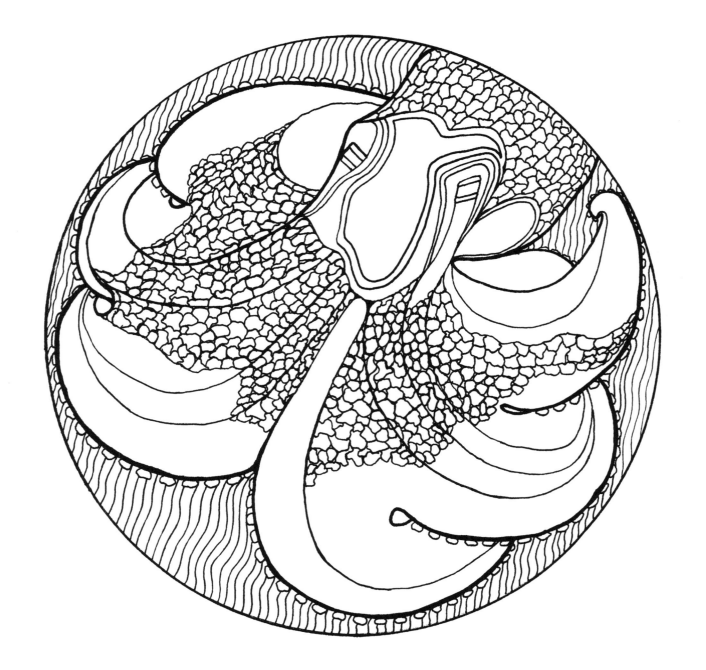

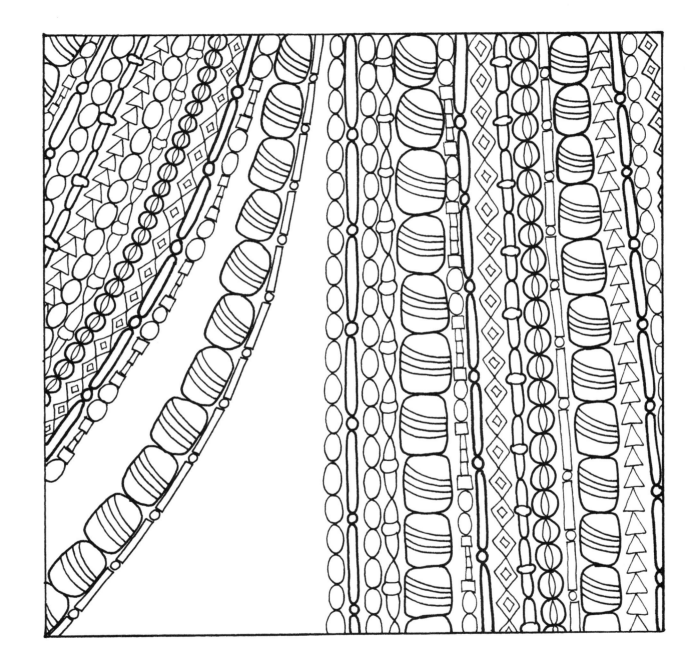

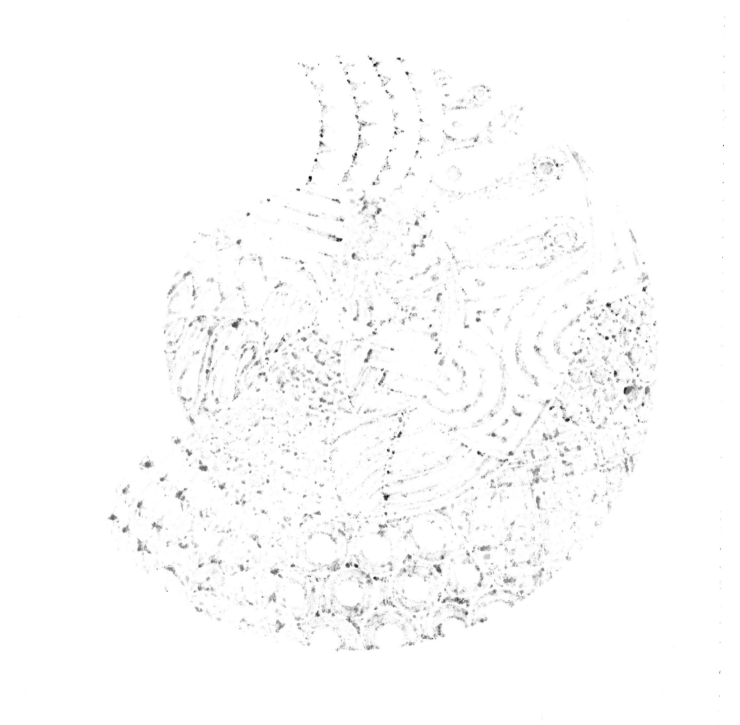

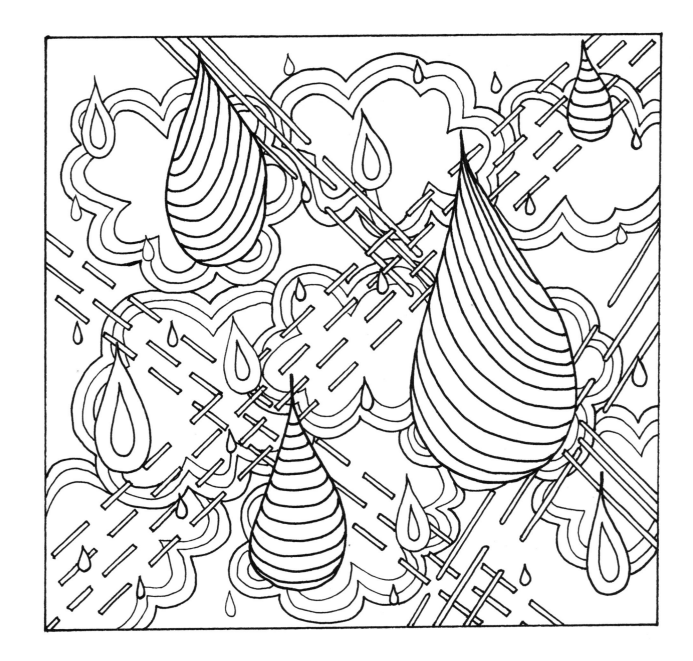

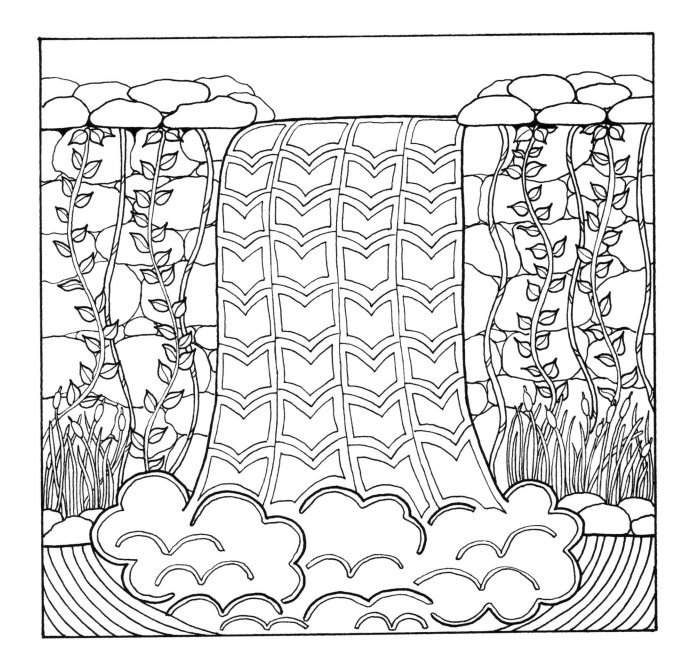

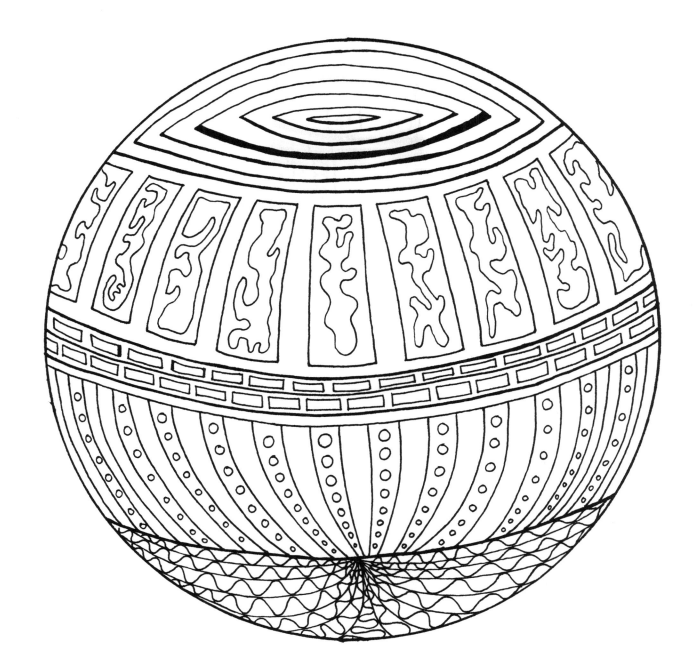

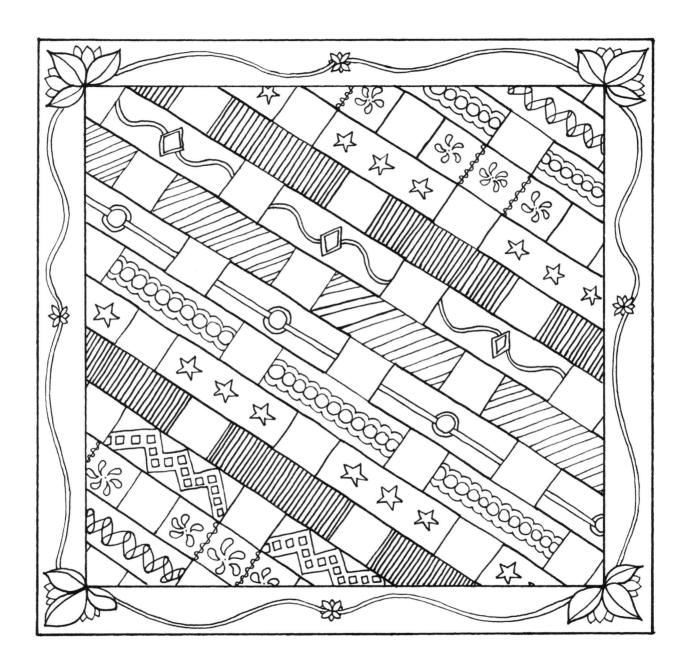

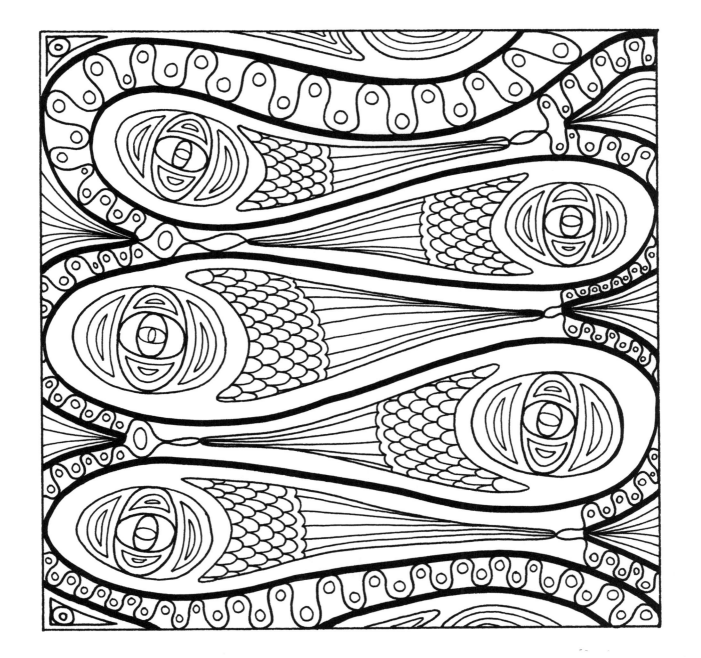

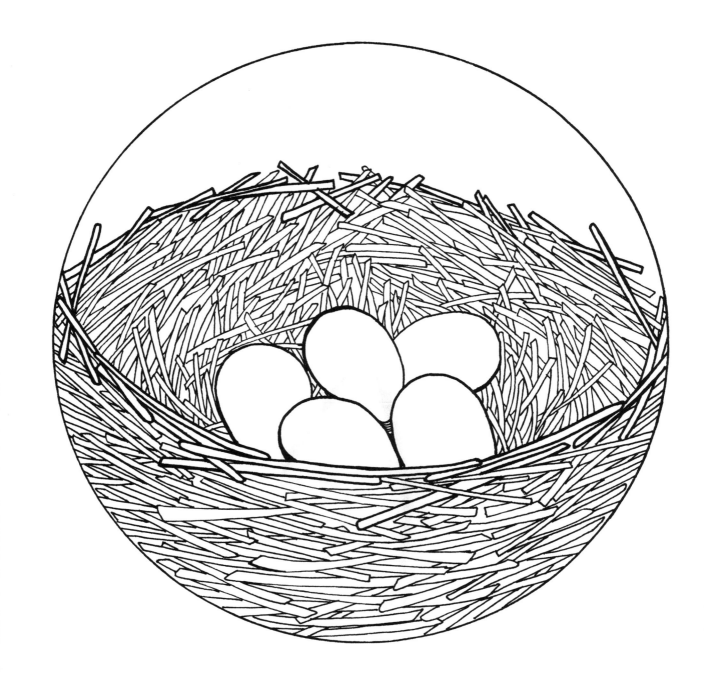

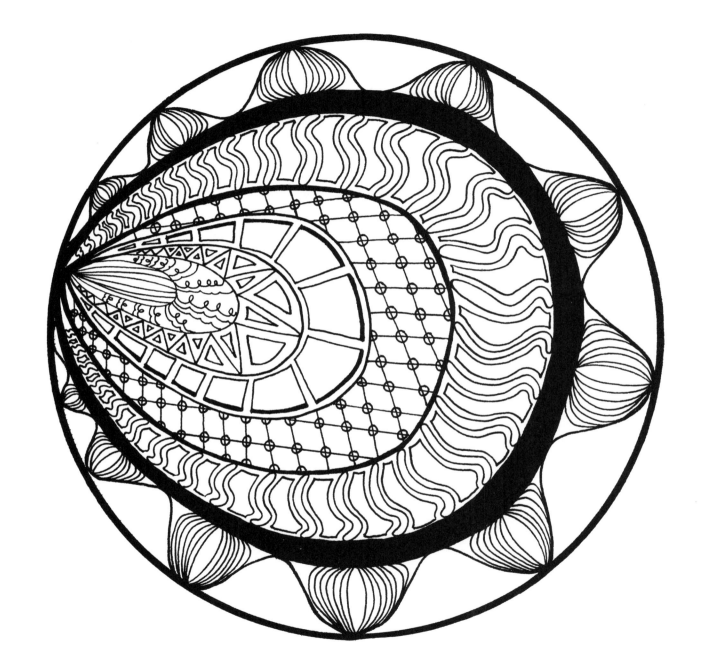

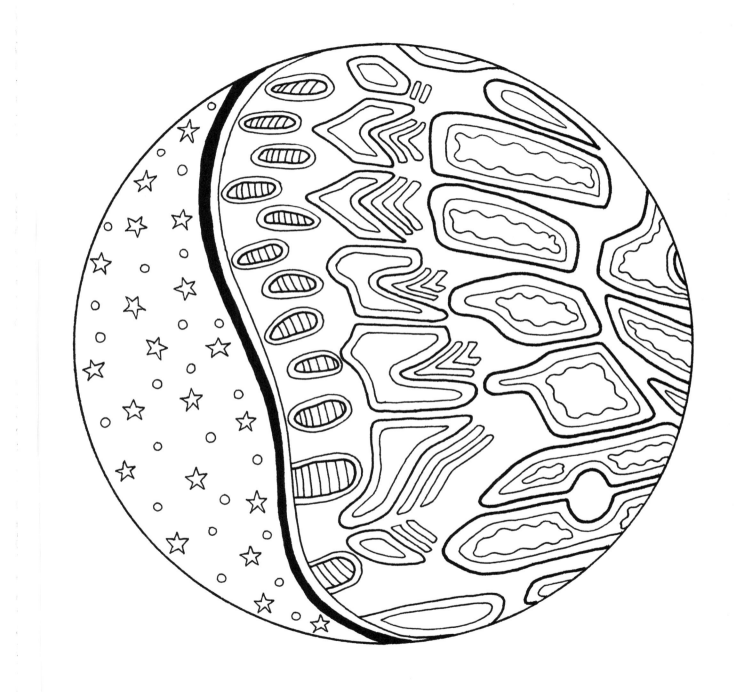

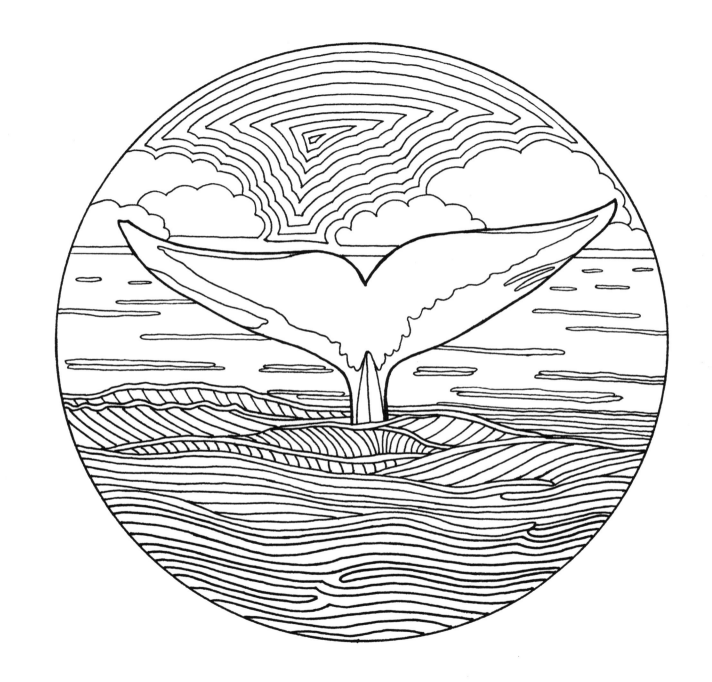

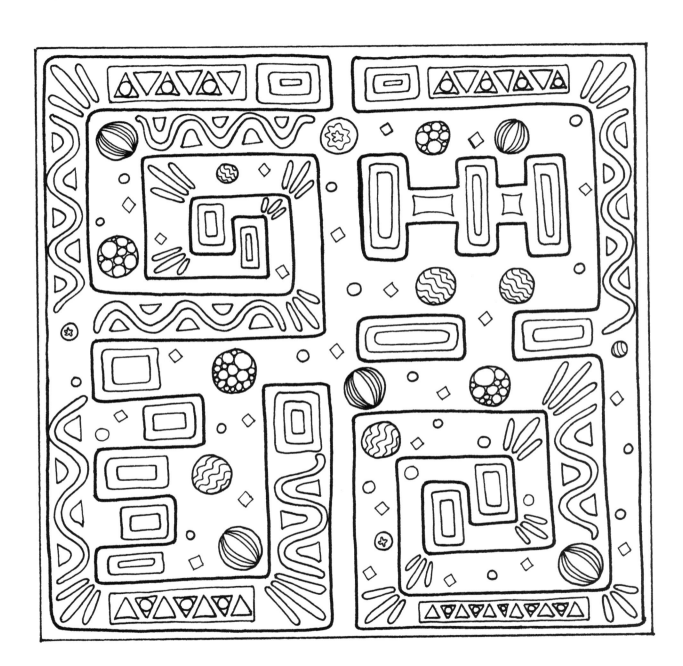

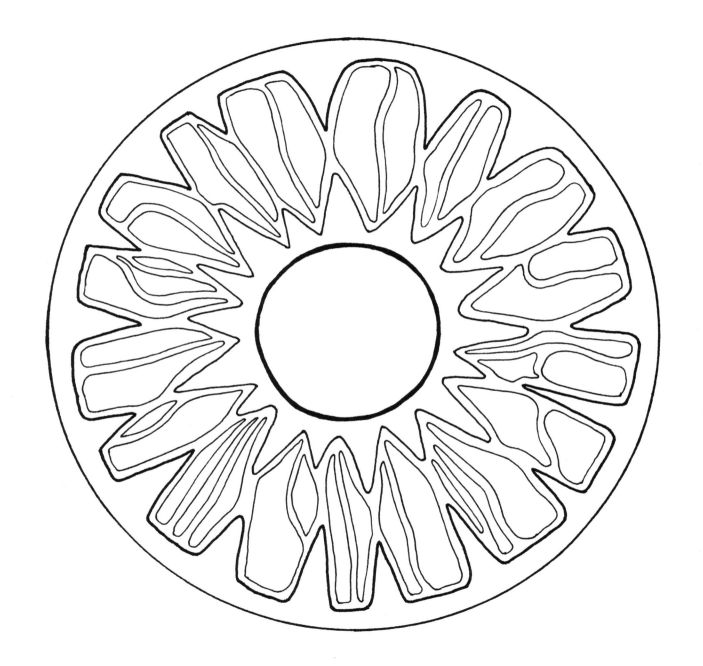

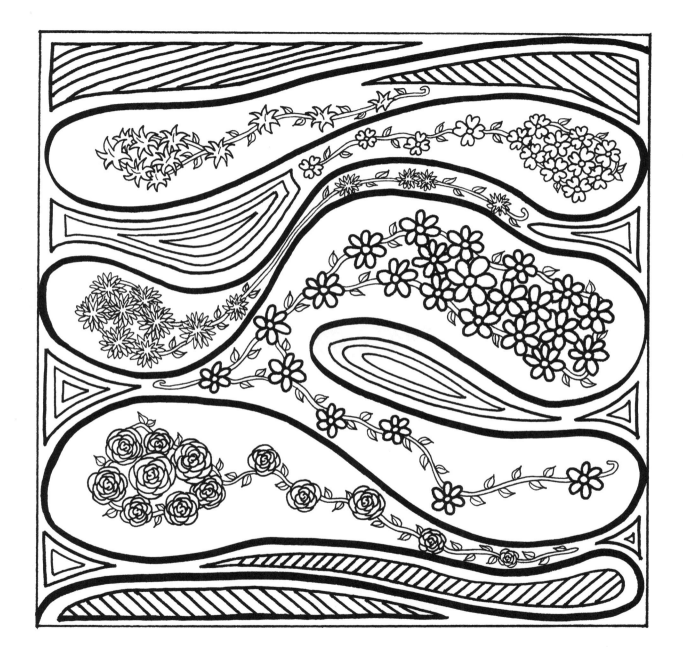

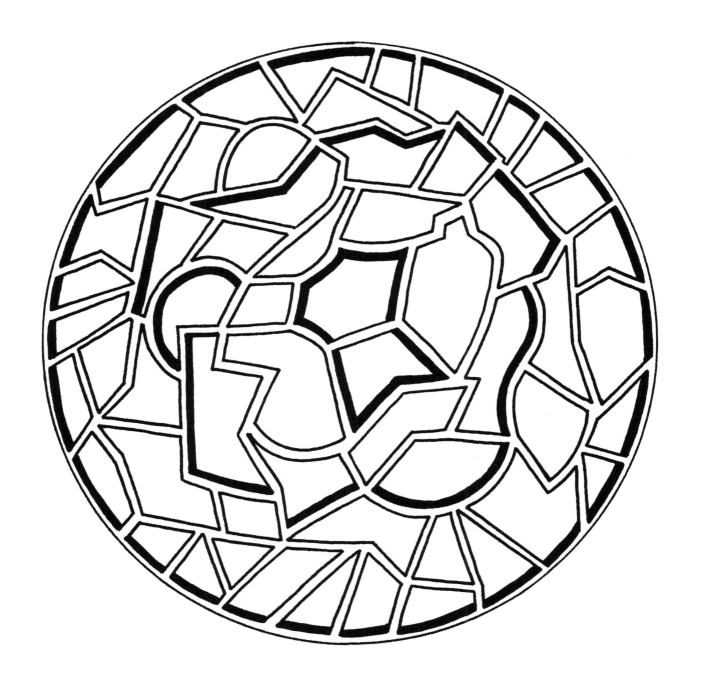

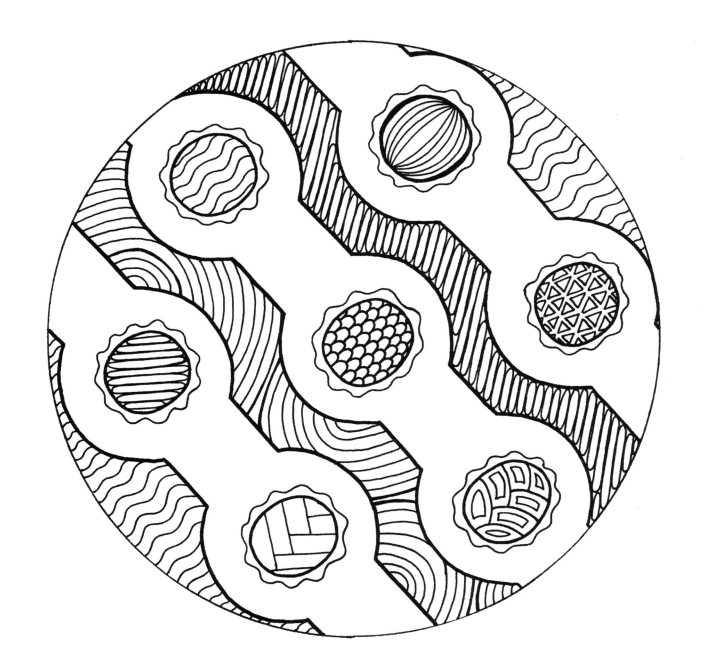

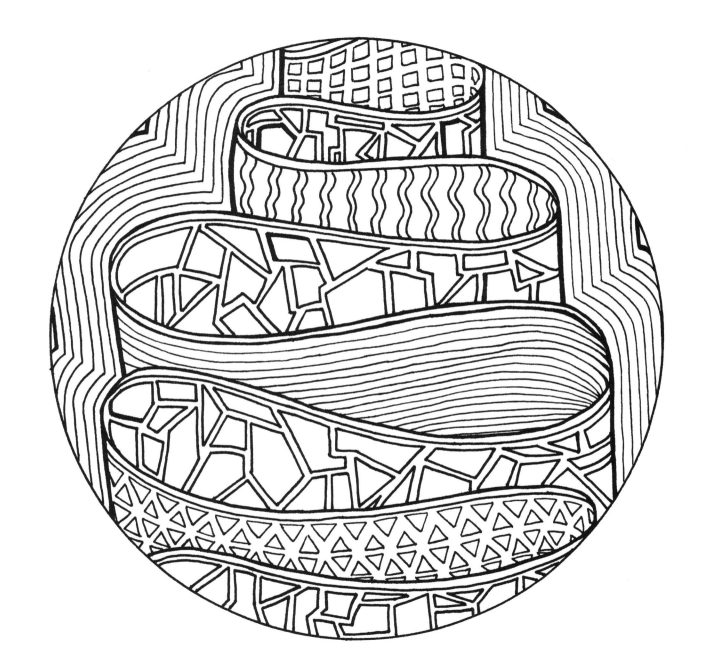

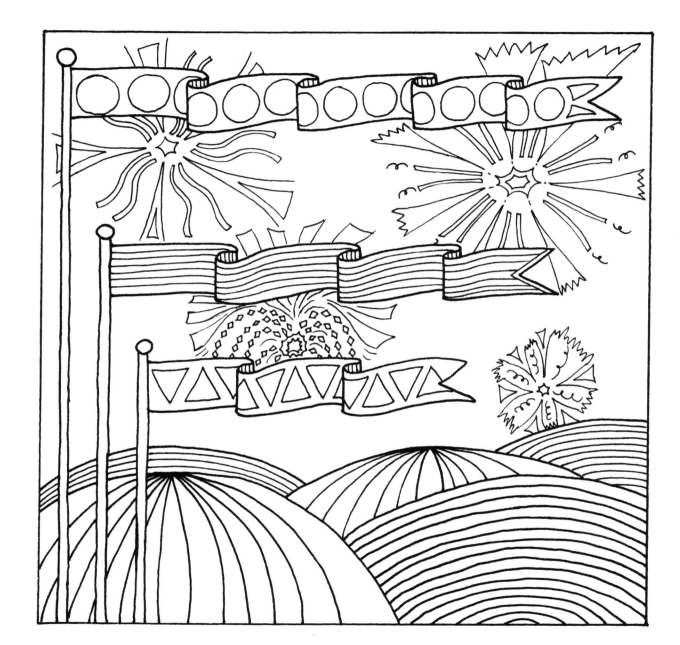

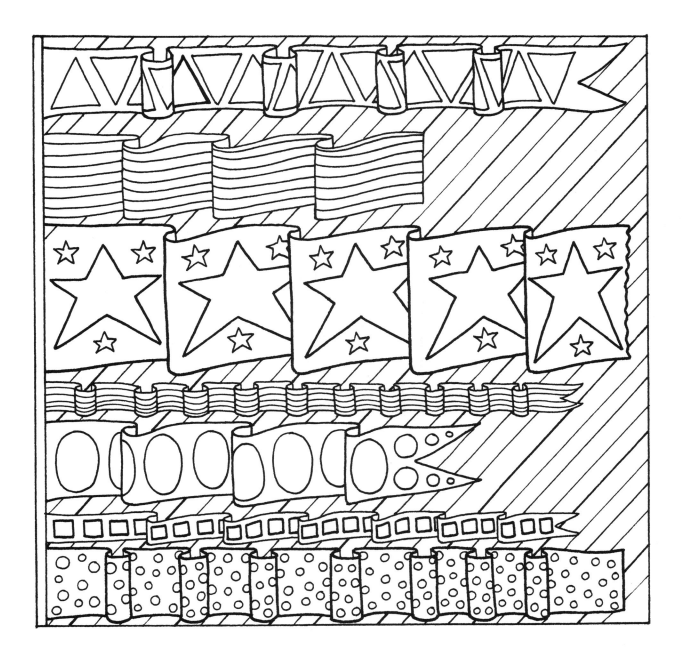

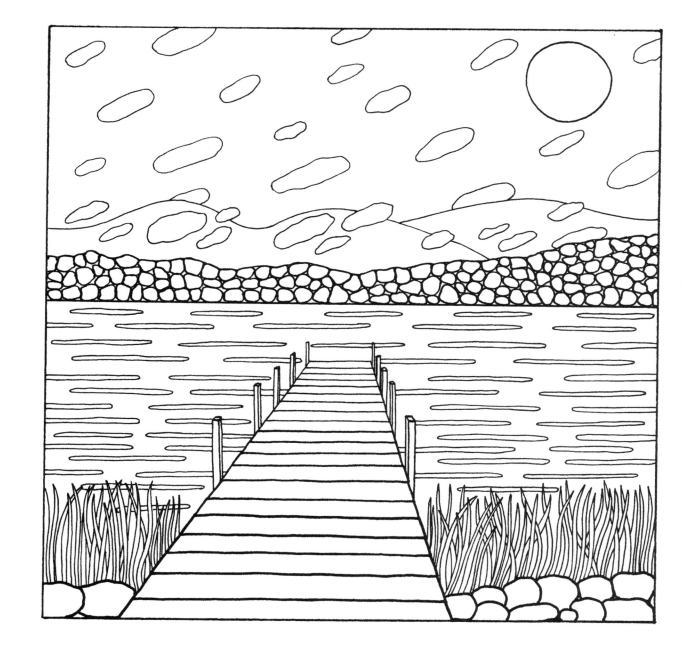